~A BINGO BOOK~

China
Bingo Book

COMPLETE BINGO GAME IN A BOOK

Written By Rebecca Stark
Educational Books 'n' Bingo

ISBN 978-0-87386-480-0

Educational Books 'n' Bingo

Printed in the U.S.A.

CHINA BINGO DIRECTIONS

INCLUDED:

List of Terms

Templates for Additional Terms and Clues

2 Clues per Term

30 Unique Bingo Cards

Markers

1. **Either cut apart the book or make copies of ALL the sheets. You might want to make an extra copy of the clue sheets to use for introduction and review. Keep the sheets in an envelope for easy reuse.**

2. Cut apart the call cards with terms and clues.

3. Pass out one bingo card per student. There are enough for a class of 30.

4. Pass out markers. You may cut apart the markers included in this book or use any other small items of your choice.

5. Decide whether or not you will require the entire card to be filled. Requiring the entire card to be filled provides a better review. However, if you have a short time to fill, you may prefer to have them do the just the border or some other format. Tell the class before you begin what is required.

6. There are 50 terms. Read the list before you begin. If there are any terms that have not been covered in class, you may want to read to the students the term and clues before you begin.

7. There is a blank space in the middle of each card. You can instruct the students to use it as a free space or you can write in answers to cover terms not included. Of course, in this case you would create your own clues. (Templates provided.)

8. Shuffle the cards and place them in a pile. Two or three clues are provided for each term. If you plan to play the game with the same group more than once, you might want to choose a different clue for each game. If not, you may choose to use more than one clue.

9. Be sure to keep the cards you have used for the present game in a separate pile. When a student calls, "Bingo," he or she will have to verify that the correct answers are on his or her card AND that the markers were placed in response to the proper questions. Pull out the cards that are on the student's card keeping them in the order they were used in the game. Read each clue as it was given and ask the student to identify the correct answer from his or her card.

10. If the student has the correct answers on the card AND has shown that they were marked in response to the *correct questions,* then that student is the winner and the game is over. If the student does not have the correct answers on the card OR he or she marked the answers in response to *the wrong questions,* then the game continues until there is a proper winner.

11. If you want to play again, reshuffle the cards and begin again.

Have fun!

TOPICS INCLUDED

Asia	Olympics
Beijing	Opium War(s)
Boxer Rebellion	pagoda
Buddhism	panda(s)
calligraphy	paper
Chiang Kai-shek	People's Republic of China
Chinese New Year	pinyin
Confucius	population
Cultural Revolution	porcelain
Deng Xiaoping	Qin dynasty
dynasty	Red Guards
Empress Wu	rice
Forbidden City	Shanghai
Gang of Four	silk
Grand Canal	Silk Road
Great Leap Forward	Sun Yat-sen
Great Wall	Taiwan
Han	taoism
Hong Kong	Three Gorges Dam
hutongs/Hutong	Tiananmen
jade	Xi'an
junk(s)	Yangtze
Mandarin	yin and yang
Mao Zedong	yuan
Marco Polo	Zhou En-Lai

Note: Some of the names have alternate spellings not shown here.

Additional Terms

Choose as many other terms as you would like and write them in the squares.
Repeat each as desired. Cut out the squares and randomly distribute them.
Instruct the students to place the square on the center space of their card.

China Bingo

Clues for
Additional Terms

Write three clues for each of your additional terms.

_____	_____
1.	1.
2.	2.
3.	3.
_____	_____
1.	1.
2.	2.
3.	3.
_____	_____
1.	1.
2.	2.
3.	3.

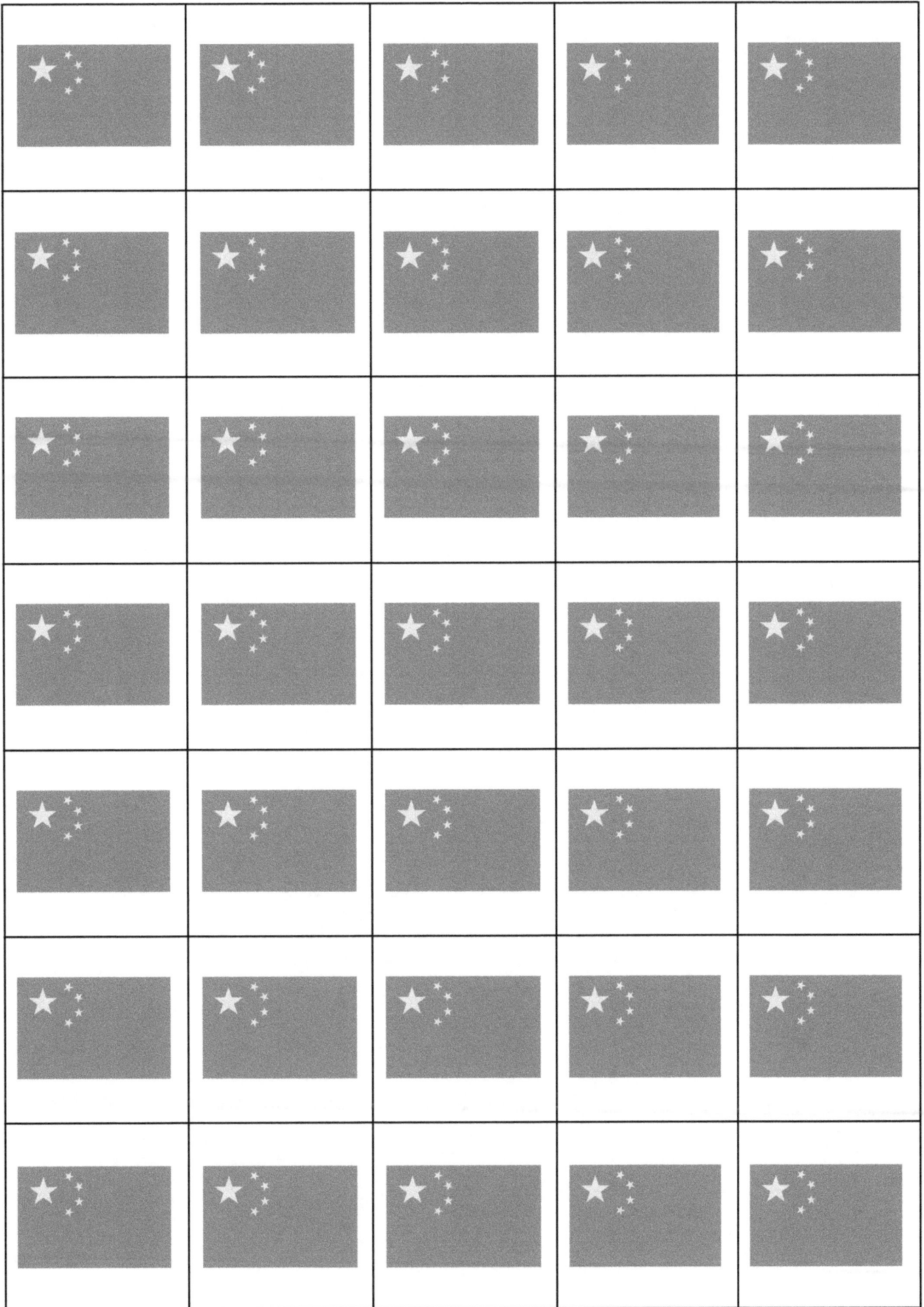

Asia 1. China is located in this continent. 2. It is the largest continent.	**Beijing** 1. It is the capital of the People's Republic of China. 2. The Forbidden City is located in this city.
Boxer Rebellion 1. It is the name given to the peasant uprising, which began late 1899. 2. The ___ was an attempt by members of the Society of Righteous and Harmonious Fists (*Yihe tuan*) to rid China of foreigners.	**Buddhism** 1. Siddhartha Gautama, who lived from *c.* 566 to *c.* 480 BCE was its founder. 2. The Four Noble Truths about suffering comprise the essence of this religion.
calligraphy 1. The word comes from two Greek words meaning "beautiful writing." 2. This elegant form of lettering is greatly revered in China.	**Chiang Kai-shek** 1. ___ was head of the Kuomintang, or Chinese Nationalist Party, from 1928 to 1949. 2. Following the civil war in 1949, ___ established a government in exile in Taiwan, which he led until his death in 1975.
Chinese New Year 1. In 2000 ___ fell on February 5. 2. People wear red clothes and write poems on red paper to celebrate this event. It is the longest holiday in the Chinese calendar.	**Confucius** 1. This teacher and philosopher was born in Qufu in 551 BCE. 2. The *Analects* is a collection of this philosopher's sayings and short dialogues.
Cultural Revolution 1. This term refers to the mass mobilization of urban Chinese youth led by Mao Zedong. 2. This movement was an attempt by Mao to reassert his authority on the Chinese Communist Party.	**Deng Xiaoping** 1. His economic reforms, known as "The Four Modernizations," set the foundation for China's emergence as a economic power. 2. He supported the forceful suppression of the protests at Tiananmen Square, which resulted in great loss of life.

China Bingo

dynasty 1. A sequence of rulers from the same family or line is called a ___. 2. The terracotta warriors are associated with the Qin Dynasty, which began in 211 BCE and ended in 206 BCE.	**Empress Wu** 1. She was the only female to be called "Emperor of China." 2. Her desire for power caused her to kill her own child.
Forbidden City 1. At the center of Beijing, it was the imperial palace from the Ming dynasty through the Qing dynasty. 2. The Gate of Heavenly Purity, or *Qianqingmen,* divides the ___ into two parts.	**Gang of Four** 1. They were convicted of implementing the harsh policies of Mao Zedong during the Cultural Revolution. 2. Among them was Mao's widow, Qing Jiang, who was convicted of inciting unrest.
Grand Canal 1. It is the longest in the world. In fact, it is much longer than the Suez or the Panama. 2. Construction of the ___ began in 486 BCE, making it the oldest as well as the longest.	**Great Leap Forward** 1. The ___ refers to Mao's attempt to modernize the economy of China. 2. Mao's Five Year Plan to develop agriculture and industry is known as the ___.
Great Wall 1. Emperor Qin had the different sections of the ___ joined together after the unification of China. 2. It was built to protect China from various invaders and extends thousands of miles.	**Han** 1. The ___ dynasty consisted of two dynasties: the Western ___ dynasty, from 206 BCE to 24 CE, and the Eastern ___ dynasty, from 25 to 220 CE. 2. Emperor Wu ruled the ___ dynasty for 54 years.
Hong Kong 1. This major city was ceded to the United Kingdom after the Opium Wars in 1842 but was occupied by Japan from the end of 1941 until mid-1945. 2. In 1997 the United Kingdom returned this city to the People's Republic of China.	**hutongs/Hutong** 1. The narrow streets and alleys of Beijing and other Chinese cities are called ___ . 2. Qianshi ___ is so narrow that only one person can pass through at one time.

China Bingo

jade 1. There is an old Chinese saying that "gold is valuable but ___ is invaluable." 2. Called *yu* in Chinese, this gem is a symbol of beauty, nobility and purity.	**junk(s)** 1. It is an ancient Chinese sailboat. 2. These study sailboats were used for ocean voyages as early as the second century CE.
Mandarin 1. There are more native speakers of this language than any other in the world. 2. Most people in the People's Republic of China speak this language.	**Mao Zedong** 1. This revolutionary was the first Chairman of the People's Republic of China. 2. A large portrait of ___ hangs at the Tiananmen gate.
Marco Polo 1. His stories of his travels throughout China became a great travelogue. 2. This Westerner served in the court of Kublai Khan.	**Olympics** 1. The 2008 Summer ___ were held in Beijing. 2. Beijing National Stadium, built for use during the 2008 Summer ___, is also known as the Bird's Nest.
Opium War(s) 1. This conflict was also called the Anglo-Chinese War. 2. The Treaty of Nanking between Britain and China ended the first ___, which was fought between 1839 and 1842.	**pagoda** 1. A tiered tower with multiple stories is called a ___. 2. Early ___ were built to preserve Buddhist relics and had many stories.
panda(s) 1. The giant ___ is native to the southwestern part of China and is protected by Chinese law. 2. Contrary to past belief, they are, in fact, related to bears. Although carnivores, they eat mostly bamboo.	**paper** 1. Although probably not the first, Cai Lun is traditionally credited with the invention of ___ in 105 CE. 2. Cai Lun created a sheet of ___ using fibers from plants, fishnets, rags and hemp.

China Bingo

People's Republic of China	pinyin
1. Mao Zedong was the first chairman of the ___. 2. It was formally established on October 1, 1949, with its capital at Beijing.	1. It is a system for transliterating Chinese ideograms into the Roman alphabet. 2. This system helps Westerners learn Mandarin.
population	**porcelain**
1. In 2009 the ___ of China was 1,334,490,000! 2. In 2009 China had almost twenty percent of the world's ___.	1. ___ was invented in China and came to be called "china." 2. In the 7th century CE, Tao-Yue used "white clay" from the Yangtze River to produce the first white ___.
Qin dynasty	**Red Guards**
1. The first emperor of the ___ unified China. 2. It was during the ___ that the individual parts of Great Wall of China were connected.	1. These militant students were mobilized by Mao during the Cultural Revolution. 2. Some of these young people became very violent against anyone who criticized Mao or his teachings.
rice	**Shanghai**
1. It is the most important crop and a staple food in China. 2. The Chinese developed the idea of growing ___ in wet areas such as river deltas.	1. With a population of about 20 million, ___ is the largest city in China. Beijing is second largest. 2. ___ is an important commercial and financial center of mainland China. Its Pudong district has many skyscrapers.
silk	**Silk Road**
1. Around 2640 BCE Empress Hsi Ling Shi learned to unwind threads of ___. 2. For about 3,000 years the Chinese guarded the secret to making this beautiful fabric.	1. This ancient trade route connected China with the Mediterranean. 2. Although it got its name from the major product traded, many other products were traded along this route as well.

Sun Yat-sen	Taiwan
1. This founder of the Kuomintang Party has been called the "Father of the Chinese Revolution."	1. Its capital is Taipei.
2. He based his idea of revolution on "Three Principles of the People": nationalism, democracy, and equalization.	2. In 1971 the People's Republic of China replaced ___ at the United Nations.
Taoism	**Three Gorges Dam**
1. Confucianism and ___, also known as daoism, are both important philosophies in China.	1. It is the world's largest hydropower project.
2. *Yin* and *yang* are important concepts of this philosophy.	2. When complete, the controversial ___ will generate eight times the power of the Hoover Dam.
Tiananmen	**Xi'an**
1. ___ Gate, or the Gate of Heavenly Peace, was built in 1417 as the main entrance to the Forbidden City.	1. Qin's tomb, an archaeological site with thousands of terra-cotta soldiers, was found near this modern city.
2. Mao announced the establishment of the People's Republic of China on October 1, 1949, from ___ Gate.	2. Known historically as *Chang'an,* ___ was the eastern terminus of the Silk Road.
Yangtze	**yin and yang**
1. Called *Chang Jiang,* or Long River, by the Chinese, it is the longest river in Asia.	1. ___ are important concepts of Taoism.
2. It and the Yellow River, or *Huang He,* are the most important rivers in China.	2. ___ are features of polar characteristics such as night and day and left and right.
yuan	**Zhou En-lai**
1. At the time of this writing, the Chinese ___ was equal to 0.15 U.S. dollars.	1. Although the highlight of President Nixon's visit was his meeting with Mao, most of his talks were with ___.
2. The official currency of the People's Republic of China is *renminbi,* but it is known colloquially as the ___.	2. The "Four Modernizations" he advocated were in the areas of agriculture, industry, science and technology, and defense.

China Bingo

China Bingo

Mandarin	jade	Mao Zedong	Zhou En-lai	Yangtze
Cultural Revolution	Beijing	yuan	paper	junk(s)
Taiwan	rice		Marco Polo	porcelain
Xi'an	Asia	Hong Kong	Three Gorges Dam	Olympics
Opium War(s)	Deng Xiaoping	Empress Wu	Han	hutongs (Hutong)

China Bingo: Card No. 1

China Bingo

Xi'an	taoism	pagoda	Red Guards	Opium War(s)
Olympics	paper	Chinese New Year	Asia	Sun Yat-sen
silk	Deng Xiaoping		Forbidden City	Hong Kong
Great Wall	Silk Road	rice	pinyin	junk(s)
hutongs (Hutong)	yuan	Empress Wu	Cultural Revolution	Han

China Bingo: Card No. 2

China Bingo

Xi'an	Hong Kong	paper	Three Gorges Dam	Taiwan
Deng Xiaoping	Beijing	calligraphy	jade	People's Republic of China
Asia	yuan		Sun Yat-sen	Boxer Rebellion
rice	silk	Opium War(s)	Great Wall	pagoda
Han	Cultural Revolution	Empress Wu	pinyin	Mao Zedong

China Bingo

rice	Sun Yat-sen	Opium War(s)	Cultural Revolution	Mao Zedong
panda(s)	Chinese New Year	jade	Red Guards	Taiwan
Marco Polo	Great Wall		Yangtze	Zhou En-lai
Hong Kong	Great Leap Forward	yuan	Empress Wu	calligraphy
Grand Canal	hutongs (Hutong)	Qin dynasty	Han	porcelain

China Bingo: Card No. 4

China Bingo

hutongs (Hutong)	Yangtze	Asia	Chinese New Year	Cultural Revolution
panda(s)	Hong Kong	calligraphy	Forbidden City	Beijing
taoism	porcelain		Gang of Four	dynasty
junk(s)	Sun Yat-sen	Mandarin	pinyin	Grand Canal
paper	Empress Wu	Shanghai	rice	Marco Polo

China Bingo: Card No. 5

China Bingo

Boxer Rebellion	**Sun Yat-sen**	**pagoda**	**taoism**	**porcelain**
Three Gorges Dam	**Asia**	**Grand Canal**	**jade**	**Taiwan**
Red Guards	**calligraphy**		**Chinese New Year**	**Forbidden City**
Empress Wu	**Opium War(s)**	**pinyin**	**Qin dynasty**	**Marco Polo**
Olympics	**Hong Kong**	**Mandarin**	**Shanghai**	**Mao Zedong**

China Bingo: Card No. 6

China Bingo

Mandarin	Sun Yat-sen	dynasty	Gang of Four	paper
Olympics	Mao Zedong	Deng Xiaoping	Beijing	panda(s)
pagoda	Zhou En-lai		Forbidden City	Buddhism
rice	Great Wall	Taiwan	Xi'an	silk
Empress Wu	Cultural Revolution	pinyin	Qin dynasty	Boxer Rebellion

China Bingo: Card No. 7

China Bingo

Marco Polo	Sun Yat-sen	Chiang Kai-shek	Three Gorges Dam	Buddhism
panda(s)	taoism	Red Guards	porcelain	Chinese New Year
Taiwan	population		Mao Zedong	Yangtze
Han	rice	Xi'an	Grand Canal	Great Wall
yuan	Empress Wu	Qin dynasty	Asia	Olympics

China Bingo: Card No. 8

China Bingo

Forbidden City	paper	Deng Xiaoping	Taiwan	porcelain
Grand Canal	taoism	Marco Polo	Asia	Mao Zedong
People's Republic of China	Mandarin		Beijing	Chiang Kai-shek
Buddhism	hutongs (Hutong)	Opium War(s)	Gang of Four	dynasty
Great Wall	pinyin	calligraphy	Xi'an	Yangtze

China Bingo

Xi'an	Three Gorges Dam	Chinese New Year	Red Guards	Shanghai
porcelain	Buddhism	jade	Beijing	Mao Zedong
population	Sun Yat-sen		Zhou En-lai	silk
Opium War(s)	junk(s)	Grand Canal	pinyin	People's Republic of China
Confucius	Olympics	pagoda	hutongs (Hutong)	Marco Polo

China Bingo: Card No. 10

China Bingo

Boxer Rebellion	Sun Yat-sen	Asia	Grand Canal	Olympics
Chiang Kai-shek	People's Republic of China	Gang of Four	Forbidden City	jade
panda(s)	taoism		pagoda	Deng Xiaoping
Confucius	Taiwan	pinyin	Cultural Revolution	Xi'an
calligraphy	Empress Wu	Mandarin	Qin dynasty	paper

China Bingo: Card No. 11

China Bingo

paper	Yangtze	People's Republic of China	Three Gorges Dam	Forbidden City
Deng Xiaoping	yuan	taoism	Qin dynasty	Beijing
Mandarin	dynasty		porcelain	Red Guards
Empress Wu	Great Wall	Mao Zedong	Xi'an	panda(s)
Sun Yat-sen	Chiang Kai-shek	population	calligraphy	Buddhism

China Bingo: Card No. 12

China Bingo

Confucius	Yangtze	Boxer Rebellion	People's Republic of China	porcelain
taoism	Chiang Kai-shek	Sun Yat-sen	Forbidden City	silk
Three Gorges Dam	Chinese New Year		Deng Xiaoping	dynasty
Marco Polo	pinyin	Buddhism	population	Xi'an
Empress Wu	junk(s)	Qin dynasty	Mandarin	Gang of Four

China Bingo: Card No.13

© Barbara M Peller

China Bingo

Cultural Revolution	taoism	Asia	Forbidden City	Confucius
Buddhism	Mandarin	People's Republic of China	Beijing	Sun Yat-sen
Grand Canal	Zhou En-lai		pagoda	calligraphy
junk(s)	pinyin	population	Chinese New Year	Boxer Rebellion
Empress Wu	Red Guards	silk	Olympics	Marco Polo

China Bingo: Card No. 14

China Bingo

Gang of Four	Forbidden City	Asia	paper	Three Gorges Dam
Boxer Rebellion	pagoda	jade	taoism	Grand Canal
porcelain	Mandarin		Taiwan	Mao Zedong
Empress Wu	People's Republic of China	Chiang Kai-shek	pinyin	Confucius
Olympics	Great Wall	Qin dynasty	Shanghai	Deng Xiaoping

China Bingo: Card No. 15

China Bingo

Chinese New Year	People's Republic of China	Chiang Kai-shek	Shanghai	Silk Road
Red Guards	silk	dynasty	panda(s)	Zhou En-lai
Confucius	Yangtze		porcelain	Deng Xiaoping
rice	Buddhism	Empress Wu	Gang of Four	Xi'an
Grand Canal	yin and yang	Qin dynasty	Great Wall	Sun Yat-sen

China Bingo: Card No. 16

China Bingo

Confucius	Tiananmen	Great Leap Forward	People's Republic of China	Cultural Revolution
Gang of Four	Grand Canal	pinyin	Zhou En-lai	dynasty
Forbidden City	Xi'an		yin and yang	Chiang Kai-shek
hutongs (Hutong)	Olympics	Marco Polo	Asia	silk
Opium War(s)	calligraphy	paper	Three Gorges Dam	Yangtze

China Bingo: Card No. 17

China
Bingo

Mao Zedong	population	Buddhism	Grand Canal	Red Guards
Sun Yat-sen	Confucius	Opium War(s)	porcelain	calligraphy
Forbidden City	silk		Great Leap Forward	Shanghai
hutongs (Hutong)	jade	pinyin	Xi'an	pagoda
yin and yang	People's Republic of China	Asia	Tiananmen	Boxer Rebellion

China Bingo: Card No. 18

China Bingo

porcelain	Boxer Rebellion	People's Republic of China	Chiang Kai-shek	population
Gang of Four	Three Gorges Dam	Shanghai	paper	Zhou En-lai
Tiananmen	Cultural Revolution		Beijing	Mao Zedong
pagoda	yin and yang	Opium War(s)	Great Wall	Great Leap Forward
Taiwan	Silk Road	Olympics	Marco Polo	Qin dynasty

China Bingo: Card No. 19

China Bingo

population	Tiananmen	Three Gorges Dam	People's Republic of China	Beijing
Chinese New Year	Deng Xiaoping	panda(s)	Opium War(s)	Red Guards
Yangtze	dynasty		rice	jade
hutongs (Hutong)	Marco Polo	Han	Great Wall	yin and yang
Hong Kong	yuan	Silk Road	Xi'an	Great Leap Forward

China Bingo: Card No. 20

China Bingo

Gang of Four	Boxer Rebellion	panda(s)	People's Republic of China	junk(s)
Yangtze	Great Leap Forward	Buddhism	Chiang Kai-shek	Mandarin
silk	Olympics		Tiananmen	Asia
Opium War(s)	paper	yin and yang	hutongs (Hutong)	Marco Polo
rice	Silk Road	Qin dynasty	Confucius	Great Wall

China Bingo

Taiwan	pagoda	Great Leap Forward	taoism	Confucius
Red Guards	Three Gorges Dam	Mao Zedong	Chiang Kai-shek	Beijing
Buddhism	Zhou En-lai		Mandarin	dynasty
yin and yang	hutongs (Hutong)	Great Wall	jade	Cultural Revolution
Silk Road	calligraphy	Tiananmen	silk	panda(s)

China Bingo: Card No. 22

China Bingo

Chinese New Year	Tiananmen	paper	taoism	Qin dynasty
Boxer Rebellion	population	Olympics	Gang of Four	jade
pagoda	Confucius		Han	Mandarin
silk	Silk Road	yin and yang	calligraphy	Great Wall
junk(s)	Marco Polo	yuan	Opium War(s)	Great Leap Forward

China Bingo: Card No. 23

China Bingo

Chinese New Year	population	Cultural Revolution	Tiananmen	Chiang Kai-shek
porcelain	Qin dynasty	panda(s)	Red Guards	Mandarin
dynasty	Shanghai		Confucius	silk
junk(s)	Han	yin and yang	calligraphy	Yangtze
Hong Kong	rice	Silk Road	Three Gorges Dam	yuan

China Bingo: Card No. 24

China Bingo

rice	panda(s)	Tiananmen	Asia	Great Leap Forward
jade	junk(s)	Gang of Four	Chinese New Year	Beijing
Yangtze	Chiang Kai-shek		Han	yin and yang
Shanghai	hutongs (Hutong)	yuan	Silk Road	Zhou En-lai
Qin dynasty	Cultural Revolution	Buddhism	Grand Canal	Hong Kong

China Bingo: Card No. 25

China Bingo

Great Leap Forward	Tiananmen	Han	Red Guards	Shanghai
Opium War(s)	Three Gorges Dam	Chiang Kai-shek	population	Chinese New Year
junk(s)	pagoda		Zhou En-lai	rice
Confucius	taoism	hutongs (Hutong)	Silk Road	yin and yang
dynasty	Grand Canal	Asia	yuan	Hong Kong

China Bingo: Card No. 26

China Bingo

Han	Buddhism	Tiananmen	population	Deng Xiaoping
junk(s)	pagoda	Gang of Four	yin and yang	Beijing
pinyin	yuan		Silk Road	rice
Shanghai	Boxer Rebellion	panda(s)	Hong Kong	jade
Confucius	Zhou En-lai	Great Leap Forward	Taiwan	dynasty

China Bingo

porcelain	population	Xi'an	Tiananmen	Buddhism
Deng Xiaoping	Great Leap Forward	Han	Opium War(s)	Zhou En-lai
yuan	silk		Shanghai	Red Guards
dynasty	Taiwan	Olympics	Silk Road	yin and yang
taoism	Forbidden City	Confucius	Hong Kong	junk(s)

China Bingo

Great Leap Forward	population	Shanghai	Gang of Four	Forbidden City
junk(s)	Opium War(s)	panda(s)	dynasty	Taiwan
Yangtze	Han		Beijing	Tiananmen
Deng Xiaoping	hutongs (Hutong)	Mao Zedong	Silk Road	yin and yang
Chinese New Year	Chiang Kai-shek	Hong Kong	Boxer Rebellion	yuan

China Bingo: Card No. 29

China Bingo

Cultural Revolution	Tiananmen	Red Guards		Yangtze
jade	Shanghai	pagoda	Zhou En-lai	Beijing
Hong Kong	calligraphy		dynasty	panda(s)
junk(s)	Boxer Rebellion	population	Silk Road	Han
hutongs (Hutong)	paper	yuan	Great Leap Forward	Mao Zedong